THE CANCER CHRONICLES

The

Cancer
Chronicles

MY ELEVEN-YEAR JOURNEY AND
ADVICE TO FIGHT THE BIG C

Mike Grasee

ISBNs: 978-1-7344742-0-6 (Pbk); 978-1-7344742-1-3 (Kindle); 978-1-7344742-2-0 (ePub)

Library of Congress Catalog Number: 2020900203
Printed in the United States of America
First Printing: 2020
24 23 22 21 20   5 4 3 2 1

Book design by Mayfly Design

This book was self-published by author Mike Grasee.
To order, visit amazon.com, apple.com/itunes or barnesandnoble.com.

Contents

Introduction ix

1. My two favorite mantras: (a) I have cancer; cancer doesn't have me; (b) Multiple myeloma has never met me. . . 1

2. Give myself up to 24 hours to feel sorry for myself. Then it's back to the fight. 3

3. Everyone has a s**t sandwich. Help those with a bigger stack of s**t. 5

4. Get people talking; it will help everyone cope. 7

5. If your saddle is blazing 9

6. Do you shoot up Rogaine? 11

7. Chemo brain . . . I forgot—what's that again? 13

8. Autologous STEM Cell Transplants 15

9. Swallow the Sun 19

10. Select your Oncologist 21

11. Select your Surgeon 23

12. Radiation 25

13. Chemo side effects 27

14. A Room with a View 29

15. Sublime Time 31

16. No Whining Allowed 33

17. Measure what matters 35

18. I decide when I go cue ball 37

19. Experiment . . . always, always, always. 39

20. Pamper Thyself 41

21. Good C-Diff. Bad C-Diff. 43

22. Shrinking? Buy some clothes that fit the new you. 45

23. Go hunting for a good will 47

24. How Not to Die 49

25. It's Never a Good Day to Die 51

26. Double Vision 53

27. Recurring Infections 55

28. Bone Pain 57

29. Parent-Child Outings are Magical! 59

30. Need a Tear Duct Exercise? 61

31. Whistle While you Work 63

32. Recognize your Silver Linings Playbook 65

33. Failure is Not an Option 67

34. Ask for Help. Your Squad is Ready to Jump in. 69

35. Navigate Clinical Trials—Step 1 71

36. Navigate Clinical Trials—Step 2 73

37. Navigate Clinical Trials—Step 3 75

38. Navigate Clinical Trails—Step 4 77

39. Retain Your Medical Records 79

40. Become a Germaphobic Neat-Freak 81

41. Destroy what Destroys you through Wicked Workouts 83

42. State Your Request 85

43. Make a Molehill out of a Mountain 87

44. Sing out loud 89

45. The Sunshine and Darkness of Dex 91

46. May you Have a Bountiful Harvest of Stem Cells 93

47. Create a Fundraising Event 95

48. When Down, Talk about Family 97

49. Develop Cali Cartel-like smuggling skills 99

50. It's a Good Day to Pick your Nose 101

51. Get a Pet. I Bet you Won't Regret. 103

52. God has a Plan. Accept it. 105

Acknowledgments 107

Introduction

It's November 2, 2008. I had been suffering from back pain for six months and am in excruciating pain. Off to the Emergency Room I go at 2:00 a.m. where I am diagnosed with Multiple Myeloma, a blood cancer that eats away at the bones. I have six fractured vertebrae, my bones appear like eerie ghosts on an X-ray, and my kidney function is poor given all the bone matter floating in my blood. Chemotherapy and radiation begin immediately. Before long, two of my vertebrae are surgically repaired via a procedure called vertebroplasty—essentially adding cement to the vertebrae to make them more resilient. I'm in the hospital for three weeks, unable to leave until proving I can walk again (with a walker).

Like many of you, I've fought hard and learned many lessons during the eleven-plus years battling cancer. After several friends prodded me to write a book about it, I realized that I could at least share my story and all the helpful tips I've learned along the way so that my experience might help other cancer fighters around the world. And it's not just my advice—it's also advice from the amazing cancer care-givers I've had the good fortune to know. Together, we can hopefully give fellow cancer fighters advice and inspiration to gut out the dark days and soar on the sunny days.

Elena, Me, Anna, Eddie the dog, Kari, Maya and Zach

Anna, Maya, Elena and Zach, Back-to-school, 2018

Kari, Anna and Me, Prom 2018

Zach as Bert in *Mary Poppins*, pulling Maya and Elena's hair, 2018

Me and Anna (age 2) finishing the Ironman, 2004.

Kari and Me, Sedona 2019

Kari, Me and "DJ" Shaq at the REO Speedwagon Concert, 2018

1

My two favorite mantras:
(a) I have cancer; cancer doesn't have me;
(b) Multiple myeloma has never met me.

Situation Summary:

Early in my cancer journey, I developed the mindset that "I have cancer; cancer doesn't have me." It was my way of acknowledging the crappy situation but also not letting cancer rule my life. If I wanted to spend time with my family, or go on a business or personal trip, I did so and scheduled the treatments around the event rather than the other way around.

A while back I was in the hospital for a three-week visit. One evening our hematologist had a serious conversation with my wife Kari and me. She said we were out of options and should prepare for the worst. The only option was qualifying for a BYTE molecule clinical trial—which was a remote possibility given my current medical condition. Kari and I understood the message and the grim outlook. Our doctor left the room and Kari went home.

I then went into "Multiple myeloma has never met me" mode. I started to think through past treatments that could possibly work again. I came up with three other treatment options. And I prayed ... not for a cure but that I courageously fight the good fight. Our hematologist stopped in the next day; she supported the three options I had thought of. She also shared results that the chemo I had been on was still working, expanding our options to five. BOOM!

Actions:

Use the mantras. Keep poking for more treatment options. If you're not wired that way, elicit the help of your squad to play that role.

2

Give myself up to 24 hours to feel sorry for myself. Then it's back to the fight.

Situation Summary

When I first got bad news, I'd find myself wallowing in the mire. That's not healthy for me. To thrive, I needed to get on with the fight. I try to not get too high on the good news nor too down on the bad news. Dealing with the bad news was the most challenging so I felt I needed the rule: I give myself up to 24 hours to wallow in the "Woe is me" and then it's on with the fight.

Actions

Develop your strategy for dealing with bad news and good news. Don't get too low or too high. If treatments are working, stay focused on how to make the outcome even better (say improving diet or more exercise). If treatments are not working, give yourself a little time to feel "Woe is me" and then focus on getting better.

3

Everyone has a s**t sandwich.
Help those with a bigger stack of s**t.

Situation Summary

By talking to others, you'll likely find that everyone has a s**t (hereinafter referred to as crap) sandwich. I've also found most people have a bigger stack of crap than I do. Helping those with a bigger pile of crap can be extremely rewarding and motivating.

Recently I met a gentleman named Shane. He could have passed as Charts from the movie *Uncommon Valor*—you know, one of the helicopter pilots who has a wicked dance to Cream's Sunshine of your Love. Shane had an equal amount of valor but faced a lot of demons which made his crap sandwich off the charts. We quickly built up a trusting relationship. The first step was getting him the tax rules related to a Go Fund Me page (I used to be a tax geek). Second, he called me to ask for help finding a safe, warm place to sleep for the night. Thanks to the crew at United Way of Dane County, he then had a warm place to stay and a warm dinner for ninety days, in a place that was out of harm's way.

Actions

Listen to fellow patients. Offer to help them. You'll feel much better and so will they.

4

Get people talking; it will help everyone cope.

Situation Summary

Hospital stays and clinic visits can be really boring. Sit and wait; blood draws; wait some more; call back to meet with doctors or nurses; wait some more. You know the drill. Since I often fly solo on the visits, my tactics include working when I can, and if I can't work, gabbing with volunteers and other patients. Candidly, any conversation is helpful, even if, on the surface, it's just politely passing the time with a stranger. Talking, being with other people, really helps—and not everyone has someone at home to talk to, so make the most of that time in the waiting room. You might make a friend, an ally, get or receive some great advice, get or receive a shoulder to lean on, or learn something fun. One caregiver and I had a multi-week conversation that resulted in one of my lines: "Happy as a clam." We both asked what that really meant. With further research I found the full saying is "happy as a clam in high tide." That made sense!

One day I did my best Patch Adams, wearing a goofy reindeer hat to clinic. My goal was to get a lot of laugh-out-loud moments. I got so many I had to sit down and take in some oxygen.

In short, everybody needs somebody to talk to.

Actions

Talk to receptionists, phlebotomists, nurses, your doctor, and become friends. They'll put a smile on your face and vice versa.

If your saddle is blazing...

Situation Summary

If diarrhea causes your saddle to blaze, here's what I recommend:

1. Stay close to the porcelain bus for the times when all you can do is smile and wave goodbye.
2. Pound the Imodium AD, up to eight a day. I've found the original brand is more effective than generic.
3. Keep your basement clean and tidy lest hemorrhoids rear their spiked horns. Use cream instead of Prep H if needed.

Actions

Jump on diarrhea symptoms early to try to minimize their impact.

Do you shoot up Rogaine?

Situation Summary

To me, the most awkward state of hair growth is the emerging state—in between bald as a baby's bottom and full head of hair. Unless you free base Rogaine, I've found no good way to deal with the in-between state, other than lots of hats … which is just fine. I make sure I have fun with hats, whether it's a Patch Adams-inspired hat or hats that have a lot of meaning to me, such as the Ironman Wisconsin hat, baseball cap, stocking hat, colorful hat, gem knit at your cancer clinic, your college logo hat.

Actions

Find the right hat(s) to muscle through that awkward "emerging hair" state.

Chemo brain ... I forgot—
what's that again?

Situation Summary

Chemo brain—the forgetfulness, poor short-term memory and states of confusion can be very real and very annoying side effects of chemotherapy. I've encountered these A LOT throughout my journey. Following are my coping methods:

1. Don't be embarrassed! I've come to realize chemo brain may be part of who I am on that day.
2. Get plenty of rest. I find limited sleep makes the chemo brain more acute.
3. Read. Any reading is good reading; more complicated texts can help use more of the brain and for me counter the effects of chemo brain.
4. Brain fitness software/apps. The activities of some apps are specifically designed to help short-term memory. I highly recommend an app called BrainHQ by Posit Science. It's a research- proven, peer-reviewed brain training app that helps chemo brain.

Actions

If you suffer from the clouds of chemo brain, get extra sleep, read, and use a brain fitness app. And don't be embarrassed!

8

Autologous STEM Cell Transplants

Situation Summary

I've had two autologous (my cells v. donor cells) STEM cell transplants as well as one "mini-transplant" (roughly one-half the quantity of my cells and one-half the dosage of Melphalan). In a STEM cell transplant, the patient is given a high dose of Melphalan to kill the existing bone marrow; then a few days later the patient receives their STEM cells and over time the cells generate a new bone marrow and immune system. The challenge is the roughly one to two weeks after Melphalan—the side effects are nasty. Nausea, vomiting, diarrhea, mouth sores and acute lack of energy are all common side effects. Patients are also at high risk of infections during this time. Here are my tips for dealing with the side effects of the transplant:

1. During the STEM cell harvesting process, I gave myself shots of Neupogen to stimulate white blood cell growth. Neupogen can cause the very strange (and sometimes painful) sensation of throbbing bones. Tylenol can help knock down that pain.

2. I decided when I went "cue ball". The first transplant I did, I waited for my hair to start falling out (it occurred during week 2 of the transplant); the nurses gave me a buzz cut

and cleaned up the gobs-of-hair sheets. For the two subsequent transplants, I shaved my head before the transplant. Okay, I'm a control freak!

3. Before the first transplant, I planned to read a lot of books and watch a lot of movies. Hah! The lack of energy and crappy state of being during the worst of the Melphalan side effects resulted in a lot of laying around and not much active brain use. I learned to accept that for the subsequent transplants.

4. Eating is tough. During the height of nausea and vomiting, I found it very difficult to eat anything. I recall looking at the menu from the hospital kitchen, agonizing over trying to find anything that sounded tolerable. Toast and dry cereal were my staples.

5. Try to stay hydrated. I received fluids through my PICC (peripherally inserted central catheter) line, which was inserted in my upper arm the first day of my transplant. In addition to IV fluids, I tried my best to also drink fluids. Water and different flavors of Gatorade were the best for me. Drinking fluids seemed to help my rumbling tummy feel a little better.

6. If your saddle starts blazing from diarrhea-induced hemorrhoids, try a "sitz" bath. This involves the nursing team hauling in a part toilet/part bath device filled with warm water and Epsom salt. It helped relieve the pain of the blaze for me.

7. Regularly use mouth rinse to help avoid mouth and throat sores, which can be very painful.

8. Exercise! Even on the worst days, I tried to get up and walk both in the morning and afternoon. My goal each day was one mile of walking in the morning and one in the

afternoon. I didn't hit that goal every day but I tried. That was the extent of my "wicked workout" but I'm convinced a little bit of exercise helps fight the good fight.

9. Remember--you haven't lived until you vomit and have diarrhea at the same time!

Actions

Talk to your medical team about their recommendations to deal with the side effects from the high-dose chemo. Do your best to eat and drink a little bit. Weave in twice-daily walks for exercise.

Swallow the Sun

Situation Summary

I can think of no better visualization than swallowing the sun, emitting its brilliant light and spawning other powerful visualizations. One of my favorite Beatles songs is "Here Comes the Sun." I try to envision *swallowing* the sun every day (that it emerges) as a way to appear and be positive. Even when the rays aren't emitting, try this visualization and see if it helps make you an energy giver rather than an energy taker.

Actions

Be an energy giver and not an energy taker.

Select your Oncologist

Situation Summary

I recommend going through an evaluation process to select your oncologist. You want to make sure your personality aligns with your oncologist's—hopefully you will have a long relationship with your oncologist. These questions, and the dialogue along the way, should give you a good sense of the expertise, personality and bedside manner of your oncologist. Following are some questions to ask to help with your evaluation and selection:

1. What are the current treatment options and related side effects?
2. Describe the journey that lies ahead? (Frequency of visits? How I'll feel? If this treatment doesn't work, what options exist?)
3. What is my prognosis?
4. What treatment options look promising in current trials?
5. Tell me about your network of Oncologists at other cancer clinics.

Actions

Ask probing questions to select your oncologist.

Select your Surgeon

Situation Summary

As when selecting your oncologist, ask questions to evaluate your surgeon. Surgery is not a common treatment option in Multiple Myeloma but it is in other cancers. In my case, I had vertebro-plasty to repair fractured vertebrae and help me move with less pain. My wife and I asked our surgeon the following questions to better understand the surgery and his expertise:

1. What are the expected benefits of the surgery?
2. What are the risks? (And in my case, why repair only two of the six fractures?)
3. Am I strong enough to go through the surgery now?
4. What are the risks if we need to use a general anesthetic?
5. How many of these procedures have you performed?

Actions

Ask questions to evaluate your surgeon.

Radiation

Situation Summary

If your treatment plan includes radiation, first go through the radiation "marking" process. Ask questions about the number and duration of treatments. If you think being still will be an issue (as it was for me: I coughed uncontrollably during radiation treatment), talk to your radiologist about the situation and your options. And last, visualize something while you are getting treatment—either the radiation blasting the cancer or a calming comfy spot.

Actions

Prepare for radiation with detailed questions.

Chemo side effects

Situation Summary

I've been on over a dozen different chemotherapies or chemo cocktails over my eleven-year journey. In general, I've responded well to nearly every chemo—often between six-to-twelve months positive response. Side effects have varied—nausea, vomiting, fatigues, diarrhea, bone pain. It's a bit like whack-a-mole—when a side effect pops up, I knock it down. If another pops up, I knock it down. The first two weeks of a new chemo are generally the worst, then I learn to adjust to it and more effectively deal with the side effects in week three.

Actions

Use the whack-a-mole approach to side effects and manage the effects better each week.

A Room with a View

Situation Summary

For those days when your crap sandwich is heaped high, you may feel like resting at home in a comfy chair and nothing more. Set up your comfy chair and lounge space to have a wonderful view. Trees, birds, water, wildlife ... whatever it may be to make your comfy spot have a great view. If outdoors and wildlife aren't your cup of tea, set up your favorite photos. Listen to your favorite music or other relaxing sounds.

Actions

Set up your comfy spot to have a room with a view.

Sublime Time

Situation Summary

It's easy to let time be your boss. I would find myself frustrated by the long wait times for appointments or treatments. My action? I talked to my PA about which appointment times had the least waits (1st thing in the morning). Then I also asked whether my transfusions for platelets or blood could be done in the Transfusion Center, a special wing of the hospital which is super-efficient. Both of those actions have helped me save time during appointments.

Actions

Talk to your Physician's Assistant on ways you can save time during your appointments.

16

No Whining Allowed

Situation Summary

A positive attitude should be an arrow in the quiver of any cancer fighter. I have a group of five friends that have run together for twenty-five years—The Running Budz as we refer to ourselves. The Running Budz have always had a mantra of No Whining Allowed to reflect that positive attitude. And what a powerful attitude it is.

One of my boyhood heroes was Rocky Bleier. He was a Running Back for the Pittsburgh Steelers in the 1970s and was a key part of four Super Bowl victories. He was undersized, some said too slow, and from Wisconsin—so I had an instant connection to him! Before professional football he also fought in the Vietnam War where he sustained significant injuries—including the loss of part of his foot. He fought back, worked his body into professional football shape and became a world champion. Rocky didn't whine during his road to recovery!

Actions

Keep a positive attitude, even on the most difficult days.

Measure what matters

Situation Summary

Following the last hospital visit, I struggled to get adequate sleep. I wandered the house pursuing meaningless tasks like stacking nearly every hard cover book in a pile to flatten a poster of our daughter's lacrosse team...Ugh! It became important to track the amount of sleep and track progress of new tactics I was leveraging to improve the quantity of sleep. Tracking blood pressure and heart rate also became important given my condition. Last, I wanted to track steps to assess the amount of exercise I was getting. The latest iWatch—version 5—tracks each of these metrics. And as any good businessperson will tell you, measuring what matters will help you focus on it and will result in improvements on that metric. (John Doerr's "Measure what Matters" goes into modifying your company's measurement and goal setting process to maximize measuring what matters).

Actions

If you want to measure sleep, blood pressure, heart rate, and/or steps, I highly recommend getting an iWatch. If funds are tight, set up a Go Fund Me page...your squad is always looking for ways to help and (I bet) would love to help buy this.

I decide when I go cue ball

Situation Summary

When "that's me in the corner/that's me in the spotlight/losing my hair" (thank you REM), I decide *when* I'll lose my hair. Consider it a regulation from the "I have cancer; cancer doesn't have me" law. That means I control the timing and the look, which I prefer over letting cancer call the shots.

Actions

Take the bull by the horns and determine how and when you'll lose your hair.

19

Experiment ... always, always, always.

Situation Summary

I constantly experiment to improve my cancer fight. From pillow-fidgeting to find that just right spot in the bed to tweaking amounts and types of antacids and other anti-nausea meds to staying hydrated without wearing out the carpet between the bed and the bathroom, I find constant experimenting helps improve the effectiveness of my fight.

Actions

Experiment in a way that would make Einstein proud.

Pamper Thyself

Situation Summary

As any parent knows, your tendency is to put your kids ahead of you. Sometimes you need to flip that and put yourself in the pole position. I recently learned that lesson the hard way. It seems odd to say, "Sorry, Elena, I'm just gassed. Can you tell me your story tomorrow? Dad just needs a break." But that's what to do when you need rest or quiet time.

Actions

Develop your words for telling the kids, your spouse or other friends, "Not now…I need a break."

21

Good C-Diff. Bad C-Diff.

Situation Summary

WTF? Anyone whose had C-Diff is LOL at the contention that C-Diff can be good. Let me explain. In a recent ER/Cancer wing visit, I stepped in at 128 pounds, well below my pre-cancer weight of 170 pounds. Surprisingly, despite a crazy cocktail of meds, I began eating like a horse. I used the opportunity to hammer on garbage calories—whipped cream, pancakes marinated in syrup, six strips of bacon per meal. Normally I was bound up but C-Diff helped me stay regular—hence "Good C-Diff." After a few days Bad C-Diff reared its ugly horns and I pivoted to full diarrhea mode. Time to load up on a med cocktail to counteract those conditions and pivot back to Good C-Diff. End result on the weight: I gained twenty pounds during the three-week stay... not bad! Not bad at all!

Actions

Take advantage of your situation. If you're hungry, pack on the pounds because you know you'll need them later. Ditto with working out—try to pack on as much muscle as possible and work out every day, no matter how little or how much you can.

22

Shrinking? Buy some clothes that fit the new you.

Situation Summary

Ever get sick of the too long/too baggy clothes? I sure did. I used to be 5′11″ and am now am 5′3″. My bloody bones are contracting plus my spine is crooked. I bought a few pants to fit the new me and it was a home run.

Actions

If you lose a pile of weight, try adding a few easy pieces to spice up your wardrobe.

Go hunting for a good will

Situation Summary

Estate law is complex and fluid. Even the inner tax geek in me cannot stay current with the machinations of estate law. I recommend hiring a good estate lawyer and making sure you have a will that aligns to your wishes and situation.

Actions

Hire a good estate attorney.

24

How Not to Die

Situation Summary

One of my favorite books is entitled *How Not To Die*. Premised on the power of a plant-based diet, it walks through cancer-by-cancer the foods that can help you avoid getting cancer and then cancer-by-cancer specific foods that can help you fight cancer. I highly recommend the book and bet you too will go all in with a much heavy mix of plant-based foods in your diet.

Actions

Read *How Not to Die* to arm your fighter spirit with specific food recommendations.

It's Never a Good Day to Die

Situation Summary

In the movie *Little Big Man*, Dustin Hoffman plays an old character who wants to die with dignity and regularly says, "It's a good day to die." While it's funny, I don't think it's true. No matter how high the crap sandwich may be, I keep fighting every day for a better day tomorrow.

Actions

Be a positive beacon on the toughest of days.

26

Double Vision

Situation Summary

Protracted use of steroids can lead to cataracts. In my case, at ten years into the journey I needed double cataract surgery due to steroids. While the surgery was inconvenient, I'm happy to report that I now have double Terminator eyes—the mechanical iris that appears as a shiny hole during close inspection!

Action

Steroid use can result in iris replacement. If you think your vision has changed, get an eye exam—an updated prescription to fit the new you may be just the ticket.

Recurring Infections

Situation Summary

Given my compromised immune system, I am highly suscepti-ble to infections. I avoid walking petri dish situations and wear a mask whenever I'm most at risk. I have also asked our entire household to be aggressive hand washers and generous users of hand sanitizer. If you know people who are not vaccinated, it's best to avoid exposure to them given the highly adverse effects of things like the measles and mumps.

Actions

Become an aggressive hand washer. Regularly use hand sanitizer. Become a germ freak.

Bone Pain

Situation Summary

Given my cancer, I've had to learn to deal with bone pain on a regular basis. The best approaches I have found include: (a) work out; (b) heating pad; (c) yoga and stretching; and (d) hydromorphone—a drug that helps douse the pain. A positive mental attitude can also help. Think of one of your most pain-filled times and tell yourself: "I got through that; I can get through this!"

Actions

Do your best to rely on non-drug solutions to deal with bone pain but use medications when needed.

29

Parent-Child Outings are Magical!

Situation Summary

Before explaining the power of parent-child outings, I should acknowledge that my family has been blessed with a good financial situation (Kari and my parents pushed us to always do our best in school, work, and everywhere else—and we've had some good luck along the way). As a result, I'm able to, on occasion, do big vacations with my family. Obviously, you don't need to spend a lot of money to have these outings, but the outings, whatever or wherever they are, really are a MUST.

Cancer has a way of interfering with life's best laid plans. One example: I planned a father-son outing for Zach, a visit to New York City to see three plays on Broadway. Acting is Zach's passion and he loves seeing plays. Regrettably, I wasn't on my A game so Kari went in my place and made it a marvelous mother-son experience.

Two years later Anna and I went to San Diego for an amazing father-daughter experience—sun, San Diego, surfing and an Ed Sheeran concert. It was magical.

That experience has now put steam in my stride that I need to complete the father-child experiences with Maya, Elena and Zach, ideally in the next nine months. (I have no plans to depart this world in the next nine months but I want to complete these experiences in the not too distant future.)

Actions

Plan and complete parent-child or grandparent/uncle/aunt-child experiences. They will create amazing memories for both of you.

Need a Tear Duct Exercise?

Situation Summary

Every so often, I feel the need not for speed (thanks Goose and Maverick) but for the need to clean out the tear ducts with a good cry. A fool-proof way to do that is to listen to the songs I sang to the kids when they were babies. "After the Gold Rush" by Neil Young, "Running to Stand Still" by U2 and "Godspeed Little Man" by the Dixie Chicks, I get a gusher that cleans out those tear ducts and I feel like a million bucks.

Actions

Ask Alexa or someone human to play the songs you sang to your children.

31

Whistle While you Work

Situation Summary

I love to work. I get an incredible spark by learning, helping solve complex problems, coaching and developing smart people who want to grow, and, when I can, moving at a fast pace. I worked long hours to make that happen. Seven weeks after I started at my company as its new president, I was diagnosed with multiple myeloma. I couldn't walk, was in excruciating pain, started on chemo and radiation immediately, and was in the hospital—away from home and work—for three weeks. I guess the pain element was like childbirth—you flush the pain from your brain shortly after the event.

What I can't flush from my memory is the flexibility of my employer and the owners. The company values included the belief that taking care of customers and coworkers would mean that everything else would take care of itself. I wasn't the first and I won't be the last employee to be taken care of by my coworkers. In fact, during my second stem cell transplant, my coworkers made an amazing AC/DC video (one of my favorite bands) that my family and I will never forget.

That is why I whistle while I work and why I try to be more Happy than Grumpy.

Actions

You're likely going to have good days and bad days, and trying to work on bad days isn't a winning equation for either party. If your employer can't offer the flexibility you need, try the gig economy and other part-time work.

32

Recognize your Silver Linings Playbook

Situation Summary

Like the movie, it's easy to dwell on the negative and miss the positives of the big C diagnosis. This may be another "WTF—I don't believe you" but I truly believe that getting multiple myeloma was one of the best days of my life because it made me a better person and has spun off a series silver linings for our family.

Here are the silver linings for the kids and Kari:

1. Elena and Maya, identical twins who love many of the same activities, developed grit like I've never seen. During seventh grade, they wanted to make a club volleyball team. They didn't make the first tryout team and took it quite hard. Then it was off to the gym to work harder. They didn't make the second or third tryout team either. They continued to hit the gym, and our driveway, and our living room to practice more and more. They made the fourth team. Way to fight hard and demonstrate grit, ladies!

2. Zach is our passionate theatre guy. Lots of community theatre, school theatre, camps, music lessons, sound recording experiences—he's all in hot committed. The one acting milestone he didn't make was participating in the local

Children's Theatre production of *A Christmas Carol*...until this year! Way to go Zach-man.

3. Anna is our hard-working high school senior. Since she was 16, she's been a Certified Nurse Assistant to get patient experience , help people and earn some money. Her chosen undergrad is micro-biology and she wants to be a hematologist. (I just paused to dry my eyes. And again.) She's got a bevy of awesome colleges to choose from and I can't wait to see where she lands.

4. It was hardest for me to think of the silver lining for Kari. There have been a host of new responsibilities piled onto Kari's already tall stack-o-stuff because of my condition. Maybe it's me being here, as engaged as possible, every day I can, that makes for her silver lining.

Actions

Think about the good things that came from your "crap sandwich" situation and I bet you'll see some shiny silver linings. Then reflect and pray on them and I hope they make your crap situation feel a little better.

Failure is Not an Option

Situation Summary

Sometimes on those hard days fighting is so hard that it's easy to consider stopping the fight. I was there once; I was in the middle of a nasty fight with roto virus and it was blitzing me. For the first and only time, I thought about requesting a "do not resuscitate" order the next time I was in the hospital. I erased those thoughts and instead remembered the attitude of the crew of Apollo 13: Failure is not an option. Their methodical approach to survival is just what we cancer fighters need—knock down one challenge, then the next, then the next. We can't think about step 672; we have to think only of the next step.

Actions

Keep fighting, one step at a time.

34

Ask for Help. Your Squad is Ready to Jump in.

Situation Summary

I've found that family, friends and neighbors *want* to help you but often don't know what you want or need. When I was first diagnosed, our kids were ages four, two, and the twins were only 1. And I was the primary cook. We started a three-days-a-week meal signup ... and the response was simply amazing. Yummy meals began pouring in and a huge stressor became a kid-friendly culinary experience where our squad's talent and time matched our need. Thanks again for all those yummy meals!

Actions

Ask for help. I bet you'll be amazed at the response!

35

Navigate Clinical Trials—Step 1

Situation Summary

The first step is to select leading cancer research institutions that you want to target. When is the right time to start chasing clinical trials? When you start running low on treatment options. Before that, it's too early; after that, it may be too late. I checked with my doctors and leveraged their network to grease the leading institution skids and make necessary introductions. My dream team of cutting-edge institutions includes the following: NIH (Nat'l Institute of Health), Penn, Mass General, Mayo, and Sarah Cannon Research Institute. To find out the leading cancer clinics for your type of cancer, you can do the following:

1. Ask your oncologist.
2. Check with the American Cancer Society or a cancer society that specifically deals with your type of cancer, in my case the Multiple Myeloma Research Foundation.
3. Review www.clinicaltrials.gov to see which cancer clinics have a bevvy of ongoing clinical trials. If travel is a concern, you can also limit the search for cancer clinics to those within your travel radius.
4. Check with any cancer support groups in your area.

Actions

Consult with your oncology team and do other research/networking to identify the leading-edge institutions.

36

Navigate Clinical Trials—Step 2

Situation Summary

Once you have determined which cancer clinics you will target, then start to build a relationship with the clinical trial coordinators (CTC) at each clinic. This step is critical as the research coordinators are the gateway to the trials. Here are the steps I followed:

1. Find the CTC's email address by calling the Clinic. Sometime the study coordinator is listed as part of the clinical trial Contact Info on www.clinicaltrials.gov but that information is not consistently provided.
2. Send the CTC an email explaining your situation.
3. Ask to consult with the Principal Investigator (aka the lead Doctor). From my experience, without a consult, you won't get very far.
4. Provide updates to the CTC as your situation changes.
5. Be extra nice to CTC!

Actions

Build the critical relationship with the clinical trial coordinators at each institution.

37

Navigate Clinical Trials—Step 3

Situation Summary

Now that you have identified the top research institutions and the CTCs at each institution, it's time to zero in on specific trials. The CTCs can help you prioritize and focus on specific trials. The qualification criteria can be rigorous. I've fallen out of more clinical trials than I've qualified for. But as Pink says, "Try! Try! Try!" Trials can be a fantastic way to live longer and advance our understanding of cancer. Each coordinator can help you zero in on specific trials.

Actions

Work with the Clinical Trial Coordinators to zero in on a specific trial and ideally schedule a consult with the Clinic.

38

Navigate Clinical Trails—Step 4

Situation Summary

I've followed a DIY (do it yourself) approach to chase clinical trials. If DIY doesn't float your boat, the American Cancer Society (ACS) or niche cancer organizations (in my case, Multiple Myeloma Research Foundation) should also be able to help navigate the clinical trial waters.

Actions

Connect with ACS or other niche cancer organizations if you do not wish to pursue clinical trials on your own.

39

Retain Your Medical Records

Situation Summary

I have found it useful to keep accurate records of not only treatments but of responses. Your cancer clinic's electronic medical record software may have a detailed system as well. Detailed records are vital, particularly if you plan to search for clinical trials.

Actions

Rely on your cancer clinic's electronic medical records solution if you can; retain print copies of your treatments and results if you cannot.

Become a Germaphobic Neat-Freak

Situation Summary

Why? If you've seen a germaphobe in action, it's not a pretty sight—hand washing, body dipping in hand sanitizer, etc. That said, it's critical for cancer patients to keep a germ-free home, particularly if there are walking petri dishes called K-8 students. Neat-freak relates to safety—think clean runways, no hurdles, easy to get from point A to point B. And plenty of no-skid socks. No slips, no broken bones.

Actions

Channel your inner MacGyver to become the best neat-freak germaphobe you can be. Have fun with it!

41

Destroy what Destroys you through Wicked Workouts

Situation Summary

Visualization is a powerful tool. Hanging in our workout room is a sign that says "Destroy what destroys you." I use that as motivation to visualize how my workouts are directly hacking away at the cancer. I also have a banner of Steve Prefontaine—one of my running idols—where he says, "A lot of people run a race to see who is the fastest. I run to see who has the most guts." The two quotes supply me with the added motivation needed to crank out a workout on even the toughest days.

Actions

Create a workout room, however small. Stash a few weights, maybe try to get a used elliptical or treadmill…you get the idea. Aim for four workouts per week, starting really slow and building from there. Even on you worst days, try to get a workout in.

42

State Your Request

Situation Summary

During a hospital stay filled with seizures, I struggled to get words out. It was just plain hard to communicate with care-givers and my family. I tried giving commands—do this or do that. That proved ineffective because my commands often didn't make sense. After some experimentation we learned it was more effective if I stated the outcome I hoped to achieve. Caregivers and family could figure out the best way to achieve the outcome.

Actions

Try the "state your outcome" approach.

43

Make a Molehill out of a Mountain

Situation Summary

It's easy for you or your support squad to make a mountain out of molehill. I think it's best to do the opposite: try to make a molehill out of a potential mountain. Use previously discussed tactics like allowing yourself 24 hours to grieve about bad news and then get on with the fight, recalling that your crap sandwich likely has less crap than others, and fighting instead of wallowing in the mire will help knock down the potential mountain.

Actions

When faced with bad news, focus on the fight as quickly as you can to roll with the changes and be a positive cancer fighter.

Sing out loud

Situation Summary

I have a lousy singing voice, except for deep Johnny Cash-like ranges. That said, singing out loud is good for the soul and the rest of the mental psych. One of the original cast members of *Hamilton* said he got better by trying to imitate specific singers—for example Marvin Gaye. He did a Marvin Gaye snippet and was amazing! I decided to build off the Johnny Cash momentum and have since added some Paul McCartney ("Let it Be") to my arsenal.

Actions

Develop an artist or set of songs where you can sing out loud. Then let 'er rip!

45

The Sunshine and Darkness of Dex

Situation Summary

Dexamethasone is a wonderful steroid for cancer fighters. It can eat away at cancers (in my case Multiple Myeloma), it can help manage side effects (which is why it's often part of a chemo cocktail), it can provide a boost of energy. On the dark side, sometimes the boost of energy turns into sleepless nights. I find trying to amp up on extra sleep before taking dex helps deal with the sleepless night(s) that may follow. Extended use can also puff me up like the Stay Puft Marshmallow Man. I can get jowls that would make The Godfather proud. I've yet to find a remedy for the jowls other than using it as a good time to say: "I'm going to make you an offer you can't refuse."

Actions

Embrace Dex (& other steroids) for all the good it can provide and manage the side effects.

46

May you Have a Bountiful Harvest of Stem Cells

Situation Summary

I've done two stem cell transplants (in 2008 and 2015) and a third partial transplant (in 2019) from cells harvested in 2015. Each time it became more and more difficult to harvest a sufficient quantity of cells. This despite using Mozobil—an amazing drug that helps separate the stem cells to enable harvesting and costs $20,000 a pop! If you too struggle with producing stem cells, I have the following advice:

1. Get comfy during the harvesting...you're going to be there a while (four to five hours at least).
2. Use a bed pan rather than hoping your bladder can last that long.
3. Get set with some great entertainment...movies, music or some serious sleep time.

Actions

If you battle with sufficient stem cell harvesting, deal with it with comfy entertainment and a comfy position.

Create a Fundraising Event

Situation Summary

Your squad wants to help but sometimes they don't know how. A fundraising event can be a fun, productive way to raise money and mobilize your squad around a single event. The year I was diagnosed, our squad organized an event called "Ride for Red" (when I have hair, it's red). We had a blast and raised over $10,000 for multiple myeloma research in the process. We are planning to organize Ride for Red Part 2 this summer, with similar goals (have fun, raise money for a good cause).

Actions

Create a fundraising event to have fun and raise money for a cause near and dear to your heart.

When Down, Talk about Family

Situation Summary

If you're having a down day and your crap sandwich is heaped high, talk about your family with your support team and care givers. I've found caregivers will naturally do this but if they don't you can seed the conversation. There is nothing like family to help you through a rough patch.

Actions

Talk about family to get through the rough patches.

Develop Cali Cartel-like smuggling skills

Situation Summary

Many hospitals frown on bringing in foods and gadgets. I say "Challenge accepted!" and invent ways to smuggle that would make the Cali Cartel proud. Favorite foods, smoothies, Dilly Bars, dumbbells or other light weights—all part of the stash that with a little inner MacGyver, your squad can become world class smugglers.

Actions

Smuggle in your favorite foods.

It's a Good Day to Pick your Nose

Situation Summary

WTF? Yes, there can be a good day to pick your nose. When my platelets are low, I tend to bleed from every orifice. "Harvesting" the nose helps keep track of what's happening in the schnoz.

Actions

Keep an eye on the nose if you are experiencing nosebleeds caused by low platelets.

Get a Pet. I Bet you Won't Regret.

Situation Summary

There is nothing better than a dog or cat as a sleeping buddy on those days when you just feel like crashing. My wife is allergic to pet dander so four years ago we added Eddie to our family—a hypoallergenic teddy bear. He is my shadow. He is my nap buddy. He loves to wear Packer and Steeler jerseys. He loves to dress up in winter woolies on cold days. He is an inseparable part of our family.

Actions

Whether you're a dog or cat person, I highly recommend you get a pet.

52

God has a Plan. Accept it.

Situation Summary

If you believe in a God, it can be hard to understand why God's plan includes your getting cancer. What good can come of the cancer diagnosis? Did I do something wrong to warrant the cancer diagnosis? Based on my "silver lining" analysis, I understand the good that's coming from my big C diagnosis. But what if someone searches high and low for the silver lining and comes up empty?

In those cases, I think it's vital that Big C fighters accept on faith that God has a plan and trust that God will take care of us in our cancer journey.

Actions

If you can't see the silver lining in your cancer fight, then accept on faith that God has a plan and will guide you down your battle path.

Acknowledgments

Here are the people who inspired me and how they did it:

Peter Drucker—for his sharp mind and fabulous "Daily Drucker" format.

Dr. Seuss—for his brilliant writing style that engages and entertains readers of any age.

Randy Pausch—who had so little time to deal with his Big C diagnosis and who spent precious time with his wife and family and was still able to tell the story of his dreams.

Rocky Bleier—my boyhood hero who truly fought back, dealing with adversity and helping the Steelers win four Super Bowls.

Robin Williams—so talented, so hilarious, so diverse, so multi-layered…we miss you.

Nathan Adrian—Olympic swimmer diagnosed with cancer in 2008 and who said in effect, "Screw you—I'm swimming anyway." Your picture is in my workout room…and your arms are probably bigger than my legs!

Jimmy V—his amazing fight, message, and legacy: "Don't ever give up!"

The crew from Apollo 13—Jim Lovell, Fred Haise, Jack Swigert, Ken Mattingly and Gene Krantz. Failure is not an option!

Kathryn Bigelow—her brilliant directing of "Zero Dark Thirty" and how Maya never quit. Strong women like you will be role models for my daughters.

Toby Keith—"Ask yourself how old you'd be if you didn't know the day you were born."

Chrissy Hynde and The Pretenders—"Now look at the people/ In the streets, in the bars/We are all of us in the gutter/But some of us are looking at the stars."

Lance Armstrong—who took a near death Big C diagnosis and parlayed it into being an elite cyclist in one of the most challenging sports of all. Live strong, mi amigo!

The Running Budz—friends for over 25 years whose ancillary activities evolved from Suzy Sightings to book clubs; at its core the Running Budz created a fire in the belly that drove each of us to new levels of personal achievement.

The staff at University of Wisconsin Hospital—the dozens upon dozens that helped me over the years with expert, compassionate care and plenty of laughs and smiles along the way.

Demco & Wall Family Enterprise coworkers, board members past and present and in particular CEO's Bill, Sandy and Sean; Nancy—my right hand; and Linda—the soul of Demco.

American Family Insurance for all your support and flexibility for Kari and our family throughout the journey. You have helped make our dreams come true.

Craig Schmidt—editor extraordinaire. Thank you for the abundance of ideas to add concepts, challenge the flow and in general increase the value to the manuscript.

The Rev. Dick Schmidt—editor extraordinaire v. 2.0. Thanks for editing with a fine-tooth comb as well as other outstanding observations to make the manuscript as tight as possible.

And last to my superhero family. You are my ambassadors of fight and fun. Thank you for being my beacon of inspiration, aspiration and perspiration. I love you!